...government of the people, by the people, for the people...

—President Abraham Lincoln, Gettysburg, Pennsylvania, November 19, 1863

DEMOCRACY
Benefits

Democracy is the most popular form of government in the world today. It provides many of the rights and freedoms that Americans enjoy.

Democracy: Benefits describes the main laws and beliefs that guide U.S. society. It explains how our government serves the needs of the people. It also looks at some of the challenges facing the United States—and other democracies around the world.

A-1

CONTENTS

Land of Freedom

Democracy is a form of government. In a democracy, the people elect leaders to represent them. Elections are free and fair. The basic laws, or rules, of a democracy lie at the heart of U.S. **society**. U.S. **citizens** enjoy many rights and freedoms. These are protected under our main set of laws, the **Constitution**. The freedom to speak about our beliefs is one of those rights. The right to equal treatment is another. It is hard to imagine what life would be like if these rights and freedoms were taken away.

Today about two-thirds of the world's countries are democracies. The United States has the oldest democracy in the modern world. It is important that people do not take the benefits of living in a democracy for granted. Many people fought and died to defend these rights. Education is one of the most powerful tools for keeping a democracy alive.

The Supreme Court in Washington, D.C., is the highest court in the United States (left). It protects people's rights.

Democracy Time Line

1690	English philosopher John Locke publishes his famous book *Two Treatises of Government*.
July 4, 1776	The Continental Congress issues the Declaration of Independence, which marks America's independence from Great Britain.
1783	The United States wins its independence from Britain.
1789	The U.S. Constitution goes into effect.
1791	The Bill of Rights is added to the Constitution.
September 22, 1862	President Lincoln declares that all slaves in the Southern states will be free by January 1, 1863.
1948	The United Nations creates the Universal Declaration of Human Rights.
1961	President John F. Kennedy sets up the Peace Corps.
1962	César Chávez and Dolores Huerta form the National Farm Workers Association (later called the United Farm Workers).
1964	The *Civil Rights Act* is passed. Dr. Martin Luther King, Jr. receives the Nobel Peace Prize.
1965	The *Voting Rights Act* is passed.

society
   a group of people living as members of a larger community

citizens
   members of a nation

Constitution
   the document that describes the powers and limits of the U.S. government

Democracy Is Born

The word *democracy* comes from two Greek words. They are *demos* (people) and *kratein* (to rule). The ancient Greeks of Athens were the first to develop their own form of democracy in around 500 B.C. Governments before this time were ruled by one person or a few wealthy people.

Athens' democracy was not like modern democracy. Athenians did not choose people to rule for them. They felt elections favored rich and powerful people. Most officials and all **jury** members were selected **randomly** from the population. Citizens voted for laws themselves. This is called a direct democracy. However, only male citizens with Athenian parents could vote.

It was not until the 1700s that our modern form of democracy came about. In 1783, the United States won independence from Great Britain. America's **Founding Fathers** then set about creating the first democracy in modern history.

The Founding Fathers wrote the Constitution of the United States. This document lists the goals of the government, and how it will achieve these goals. One of these goals is that the government should protect the rights and freedoms of its citizens.

The people of France watched with great interest when the thirteen American colonies declared independence from Great Britain. They were also upset with their rulers. In 1789, they forced the French King Louis XVI from his throne (above). A new government was then set up based on the principles of democracy.

PROFILE

John Locke 1632–1704

America's founders were influenced by a philosopher named John Locke (right). Locke believed that all people were, by nature, free and equal. No one had the right to harm another's life, freedom, or property—and that included the government. He also believed that people should be able to choose who rules over them. They should also have the right to replace any government that does not protect the rights of its citizens.

Locke's book *Two Treatises of Government* (1690) was a favorite of Thomas Jefferson. Many of Locke's ideas inspired Jefferson when he was writing the Declaration of Independence.

A-5

Legal Protection

A law is a rule made and enforced by a government. Many rulers throughout history made their own laws. The people had no say. In a democracy, citizens may vote for their lawmakers. This gives them a voice in the laws. Also, everyone must obey a clear set of laws, even a country's leaders. This is called the rule of law.

The Constitution is the most powerful law in the United States. It gives everyone equal protection. For example, treating someone differently because of their race is unconstitutional. This means it does not follow the laws in the Constitution.

The people elected into the legislative branch of government have the power to make, change, and approve laws. The judicial branch is made up of local and national judges. These judges decide if someone has broken a law. The legislative and judicial branches work separately, but both make sure that laws serve and protect the people.

U.S. Capitol

Legislative
Congress
The House
The Senate

The White House

Executive
President
Vice President

U.S. Supreme Court

Judicial
Supreme Court

The government is made up of three branches (left). Each branch has separate powers. The powers of each branch are designed to check and balance the powers of the others. The judicial branch is independent of the other two branches. It is headed by the U.S. Supreme Court. The president and Congress must accept Supreme Court decisions.

The U.S. Supreme Court is the most powerful court in the United States. Its judges decide if people, companies, and even the government are following the law. They must look at past and present laws when making a ruling, or decision. Since they are the highest court, all other judges and states are expected to follow their decisions.

CASE STUDY

A Balancing Act

The police must balance people's basic rights with the need to keep law and order. The rules may seem clear. For example, the police cannot enter a person's home unless they get permission from the courts. However, the line between maintaining order and personal freedoms is not always so easy to see.

After the attacks on the World Trade Center and Pentagon in 2001, the government passed a law called the *Patriot Act*. The law gave the government more powers to search for people who might want to hurt Americans. Some people say the *Patriot Act* takes away too many rights from citizens. Others say the *Patriot Act* is needed to keep the nation safe.

Serving the People

In Athens, in ancient Greece, everyone met in one place to make political decisions. The United States was too large for this form of direct democracy to work. The Founding Fathers decided it was better if people elected fellow citizens to represent them. This is called a representative democracy.

In a representative democracy, citizens vote for people to represent them and run the government. Citizens expect their elected officials to vote and act in a certain way. If the officials don't follow through, the voters will probably support new leaders in the next election. This keeps officials listening to the needs of their voters.

Vice President Al Gore (bottom, left) and George W. Bush (top, left) were both running for president in 2001. Some people said that not all of Florida's votes had been counted because of a problem with the voting machines. This could change the results of the election. The U.S. Supreme Court was asked to make a decision. It declared Bush the winner after more than five weeks of debate.

House of Representatives
a part of Congress whose members suggest and vote on laws

Each state votes for representatives to serve them. The **House of Representatives**, often called the House, is made of elected representatives from each state. The more people in a state, the more representatives that state has in the House. These representatives travel to Washington, D.C., to vote and speak for their voters.

CASE STUDY

Majority Rule

Majority rule means that decisions are supported by most of the voters, or most of their representatives. Elected officials—from mayors to the president—should support the views of the majority of voters.

Officials elected as representatives discuss and vote on issues together. Men and women in Congress vote on many issues each year (above). In this way, majority rule also determines which laws are passed.

Political Parties

A political party is an organization made up of people with similar ideas on how a country should be run. Political parties are a link between the government and individual citizens. Political parties often have different and opposing views on how best to run the nation.

The two main political parties in the United States today are the Democratic and Republican parties. The Democratic Party was founded by Thomas Jefferson in 1792. Jefferson set up the party to fight for the Bill of Rights. Democrats often promote social programs. For example, many democrats believe that the government should provide medical and economic support to those in need.

The Republican Party was founded in the early 1850s by people against slavery. Abraham Lincoln became the first Republican president in 1860. Many Republicans today **emphasize** national security. Most Republicans also believe the government should put fewer restrictions on business. However, members of both parties share a lot of the same patriotic values.

The Democratic Party symbol is a donkey (left). Democrats see a donkey as being humble and courageous.

The Republican Party symbol is an elephant (left). Republicans see the elephant as strong and intelligent.

A person does not need to belong to a political party to run for office. He or she can run as an independent. Running a campaign costs a great deal of money, though. It can be hard raising enough money without belonging to a major party.

Parties hold conventions, or large gatherings, like the one below to prepare for elections.

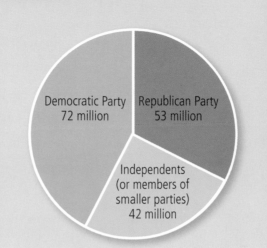

Americans Signed Up to Vote (2004)

Democratic Party
72 million

Republican Party
53 million

Independents
(or members of
smaller parties)
42 million

emphasize
feature or give importance to

candidate
a person who is working to get elected

Parties for the People

People can choose which party they want to support. The Democratic and Republican parties dominate U.S. politics. However, there are more than just two political parties in the United States. The Libertarian Party is one of the country's more successful small parties. Its members support reducing the role of government in society.

The Green Party is another small party that is gaining popularity. It promotes peace among nations and care for the environment. If people vote for a smaller party, they may impact the selection of a larger party's **candidate**. This can have a big effect on election results, especially if the race between the two major candidates is close. Citizens are also free to vote for candidates from different parties for different positions.

Personal Freedoms

American citizens are given many rights and freedoms under the Constitution's Bill of Rights. One of the most important of these is freedom of speech. A person is free to talk or write about his or her personal views on any issue. It does not matter if other people disagree. People are also free to speak out against the government.

Freedom of speech does have its limits. It cannot be used as an excuse for violence or for a false attack on someone's good name.

Other rights and freedoms guaranteed by the Constitution include:

- freedom of religion;
- the right to an education;
- freedom to gather with, and to join, groups;
- freedom to work and live where you choose;
- the right to ask the government to change;
- the right to a trial by jury.

The Statue of Liberty in New York Harbor was a gift to Americans from the people of France in 1886. It stands for freedom and democracy.

Map of Press Freedom around the World (2007)

KEY

Less restraints

More restraints

NORTH AMERICA

SOUTH AMERICA

EUROPE

ASIA

AFRICA

AUSTRALIA

publish

to make public by printing in a book, magazine, newspaper, or electronic media

In the United States, people are free to share their opinions in public. People often gather to show their opinion on what the government should do (above). This often happens when the government is making a decision, such as whether to go to war or change a law.

Freedom of the Press

In the United States, the press, or those who report the news, are free to write the facts they discover. They are also free to write their opinions. A free press is protected under the Constitution. This means that the government cannot force newspapers to **publish** articles. It also cannot stop journalists from reporting about important public issues.

The press helps keep government officials honest and fair. It also gives the public information it needs to make informed decisions. Freedom comes with responsibilities. Journalists have a duty to give true and balanced reports. They should also not release information that may place the public or the government in danger.

Changes and Challenges

The United States' government will always have the responsibility to serve its people. However, the needs of the people have changed over the years. As the country changes and becomes more diverse, laws must adapt to allow for new rights and freedoms. Each day, the United States is faced with new challenges for serving and protecting its citizens.

Throughout the years, laws to protect the rights of citizens have had a big effect on the nation. Laws have been added to allow more people to vote and to receive education. Laws have been passed to protect the freedom of citizens from abuses of power in the government. Freedom is as essential to democracy today as it was when the Founding Fathers first wrote the Bill of Rights.

Loving v. Virginia was a case before the Supreme Court in 1967. Two people of different races got married (left). However, the Virginia state court ruled they could not be married because they were of different races. The Supreme Court ruled that they could be married and ended all race-based laws on marriage.

The First Amendment is also the first right listed in the Bill of Rights. It gives citizens the right to say whatever they think is true. Many people believe it is the most important right for a free society.

CASE STUDY

Amendments

Amendments are laws added to a constitution. Amendments are called bills before they become official. An amendment must be approved by two-thirds of Congress. Two-thirds of the House and two-thirds of the Senate must agree to pass it. Then three-fourths of the states must agree to the amendment.

The first ten amendments to the U.S. Constitution were called the Bill of Rights. Many other very important amendments were added later. For example, the Fifteenth Amendment declares that the government cannot ban a person from voting because of race. The Nineteenth Amendment states that women have the right to vote.

Benefits

Democratic principles and values help shape what it means to be an American citizen. Democracy: Benefits looks at some of the key principles guiding life in the United States, and it shows how our government is designed to benefit all citizens.

1. What is the difference between the representative democracy of the United States and the direct democracy of the ancient Greeks? Why did America's founders not follow the Greek form of democracy?

2. Using Democracy: Benefits as a reference, list five rights and freedoms that are guaranteed under the U.S. Constitution. Which one of these rights and freedoms do you think is most important? Why?

3. Many countries in the world do not have a free press. Reporters are pressured to write stories that the government wants. A free press is one of the key freedoms listed in the U.S. Constitution. Imagine that the government controlled all the news in your state.
   - Would you feel like you could trust the stories you read in the news? Why or why not?
   - How would this affect you and your community?

The benefits of democracy cannot be taken for granted—they have to be worked for. And the work is never done.

—Deputy Secretary-General of the United Nations, Mark Malloch Brown, 2004

DEMOCRACY
Responsibilities

Democracy is the most popular form of government in the world today. It provides many of the rights and freedoms that Americans enjoy.

Democracy: Responsibilities describes the duties of U.S. citizens, and why these duties are so important. It also looks at the ways individuals can help us improve life in the United States and around the world.

CONTENTS

Freedom Calls

"Ask not what your country can do for you, ask what you can do for your country." U.S. President John F. Kennedy said these famous words in 1961. He was reminding Americans that the rights and freedoms they enjoy come with important responsibilities. Citizens have **civic** duties to the country as a whole. Freedom and responsibility go hand-in-hand. A democracy cannot run properly without them.

In a democracy, citizens' duties include voting in elections, paying **taxes**, and obeying laws. A democracy works when citizens respect human rights and **commit** to serving the community. A democratic government can only do so much to help a country reach its potential. It is up to a country's citizens to work together to do the rest.

César Chávez spent more than 30 years campaigning for the rights of farm workers (left).

Democracy Time Line

1690	English philosopher John Locke publishes his famous book *Two Treatises of Government*.
July 4, 1776	The Continental Congress issues the Declaration of Independence, which marks America's independence from Great Britain.
1783	The United States wins its independence from Britain.
1789	The U.S. Constitution goes into effect.
1791	The Bill of Rights is added to the Constitution.
September 22, 1862	President Lincoln declares that all slaves in the Southern states will be free by January 1, 1863.
1948	The United Nations creates the Universal Declaration of Human Rights.
1961	President John F. Kennedy sets up the Peace Corps.
1962	César Chávez and Dolores Huerta form the National Farm Workers Association (later called the United Farm Workers).
1964	The *Civil Rights Act* is passed. Dr. Martin Luther King, Jr. receives the Nobel Peace Prize.
1965	The *Voting Rights Act* is passed.

civic
having to do with the general public and its activities or needs

taxes
money people must pay to a government

commit
promise

B-3

Getting Involved

Some people are worried that Americans have become less involved in politics over the years. Only 136 million out of 201 million U.S. citizens were **registered** to vote in 2006. Of the 136 million who were registered, only 96 million actually voted. That is just 48 percent of voting-age citizens.

Almost half of the people who were not registered to vote in 2006 said they had little interest in the election or politics. Others said they were not **eligible** to vote or they didn't know how to register. Many who were registered said that they were too busy to vote.

The people who are elected make decisions that affect the lives of everyone in the United States. This is why voting is so important. Voting is not the only way people can **participate** in politics. People can join political parties. They can sign petitions (group requests for change), attend meetings, and write letters to officials. They can even run for political office themselves.

Good Habits Start Young

A person must be at least eighteen years old to vote in the United States, but they can learn about it when they are younger. Young people are more likely to vote if they have seen their parents vote. They are also more likely to keep voting throughout their lives if they start voting soon after they are eligible.

A young girl learns about voting by participating in a class election (right).

A student shows some of the trash she pulled from a local river at an Earth Day event in Virginia.

CASE STUDY

Project Citizen

Is the stream near your house looking dirty? Maybe there are no basketball courts in your neighborhood for students to play on. Every community has its problems. Sometimes people feel as if there is nothing they can do. However, each citizen has the power and responsibility to look after their community. That is one of the key messages of Project Citizen.

The project began in 1995 as a way to help young people get involved in local and state government. Students learn how important it is to help their communities. They also learn how to stand behind their ideas and beliefs. They feel good about themselves because they are making a difference.

Making a Difference

In 1835, a French politician named Alexis de Tocqueville (ah lehk SEE duh TOHK vihl) wrote a book called *Democracy in America*. He supported individual rights, but he warned that people should not ignore their communities. People need to balance their own interests with the interests of the community. Individuals who work for the common good are part of a strong, healthy democracy.

The United States is lucky to have many people who volunteer for local organizations. Volunteers can have a big impact on their community. In 2001, some 44 percent of adults in America volunteered for various types of service. Their combined efforts were equal to more than nine million full-time workers. Volunteer work can range from coaching a local sports team to serving food at a local soup kitchen. The type of volunteer work available is seemingly endless.

Governor Arnold Schwarznegger of California thanks the state's National Guard (above). The Guard helped communities in southern California recover from wildfires in October 2007.

Each year, thousands of volunteers help feed the hungry at soup kitchens and food banks around the country.

César Chávez led many protests during his life. He showed that citizens have the power to change laws and raise public awareness on important issues.

"**National Service recognizes a simple but powerful truth—we make progress not by governmental action alone, but we do our best when the people and their government work... in genuine partnership.**"

—President Bill Clinton, 1993

PROFILE

César Chávez 1927–1993

César Chávez (above) was a Mexican American farm worker from Arizona. His family moved all around the Southwest to find work picking fruit and vegetables. The pay and conditions were poor. Chávez left school early to help support his family. Later, he started speaking out about the poor conditions farm workers faced.

Chávez and Dolores Huerta set up a union to fight for farm workers' rights. Chávez used peaceful protests and strikes to get his point across. He even went 36 days without food in 1988. He wanted people to know about the harmful effects of insect sprays on farm workers. His efforts improved the lives of farm workers all over the country. Chávez was awarded the highest civilian honor in the United States, the Medal of Freedom.

Citizens and the Law

In a democracy, citizens vote for leaders to represent them. The laws of a country should reflect the views of the people. Each person is expected to obey the laws where he or she lives. Laws should be made for the benefit and well-being of individuals and society.

What happens if laws are unjust, or unfair? Do citizens have a responsibility to speak out against them? Rules made by an elected government must be obeyed. It does not matter if someone considers the laws unfair. However, citizens have the right to challenge an unjust law.

Many people have protested laws because they felt strongly that the laws were unjust. American civil rights leader Dr. Martin Luther King, Jr., was arrested for leading a protest for African American rights in Alabama. He accepted the punishment without a fight. He believed it was his duty to speak out against unfair laws.

American writer Henry David Thoreau was jailed in 1846 (above). Thoreau was protesting against the government's support of slavery and the Mexican-American War. He later wrote about the duty people had to protest against an unfair government. He called this "civil disobedience." Thoreau inspired Martin Luther King, Jr.

Rosa Parks (left) was arrested in 1955 for refusing to give up her seat on a bus to a white man. Her arrest in Montgomery, Alabama, set off a successful boycott of the city's buses.

"Our lives begin to end the day we remain silent on things that matter."

—Dr. Martin Luther King, Jr.,
American civil rights leader

Martin Luther King, Jr., received the Nobel Peace Prize in 1964 for his role in the Civil Rights Movement.

CASE STUDY

Civil Rights

The Constitution guarantees every citizen the right to vote no matter what their race or skin color. Our laws guarantee all children equal access to education. Citizens are also guaranteed equal protection. Up until the mid-1960s, some states chose to ignore these national laws. States in the South continued to follow their own laws. Some of these laws treated African Americans unfairly.

Dr. Martin Luther King, Jr., and other civil rights' leaders led a movement in the late 1950s and 1960s to fight for the equal rights of African Americans. King used nonviolent protests to bring attention to the issues. His brave efforts led to the *Civil Rights Act* and the *Voting Rights Act*.

Calls to Duty

Obeying the law is only one legal duty that all citizens share. Citizens can also be called upon to serve on a jury in court. Juries decide if a person is guilty or not guilty of a crime. It is a serious responsibility. A jury's decision can change a person's life forever. Some groups do not have to serve on a jury. They include members of the armed forces on active duty.

The many public services that the government provides are expensive. Citizens have a duty to pay taxes to the government for its services. The government would not be able to pay for services such as public roads, schools, or public safety without this money.

During times of war, citizens may be called upon by the government to serve in the military. Many men and women join the military during times of peace, too. They believe it is an honor and a duty to serve their country.

Sometimes a jury needs more information before it can make a decision. People may be called to court to testify, or tell what they know, during a trial.

There are different types of taxes. A sales tax is included in the price of goods and services. Almost all citizens must pay an income tax, which is a portion of their earnings. A mother teaches her daughter about taxes (below).

Men and women all over the nation serve in the U.S. Armed Forces.

> **A**ll the day long, whether rain or shine, she's a part of the assembly line, she's making history, working for victory, Rosie the Riveter …"
>
> —song lyrics from "Rosie the Riveter," by Redd Evans and John Jacob Loeb, 1942

We Can Do It!

Joining the War Effort

U.S. citizens have a duty to protect and defend their country if it is under threat. All young men eighteen and over can be called on by the government to serve in the armed forces during a war. In times of war, there are many ways that all citizens can help out at home.

During World War II (1939–1945), there was a huge shortage of workers in the United States. Many men had left to serve as soldiers in the war. The government put up posters of "Rosie the Riveter" saying "We Can Do It!" to inspire women (above, right). Millions of women began doing the jobs left open by the men. Some women worked with men in factories building weapons and aircraft.

Going Global

Technology has made communication between countries quicker and easier. People can find out the latest news about a country with a few clicks of a computer mouse. They can buy goods from the other side of the world at their "local" store. Many people are now "citizens of the world."

People are often told they have duties to their own country, but what about to the rest of the world? The actions of citizens in one country can affect the citizens of another country. It is important that people know the effects they are having on people around the world and on the Earth itself.

"Global citizens" are people who work to make the world a better place. They respect the world's **diverse** cultures. They also recognize people's **universal** human rights. There are many ways to be a good "global citizen." Learning about important issues such as poverty and pollution is a good place to start.

The United States sends money and people to countries hit by disasters, such as floods. This volunteer is rebuilding homes in India destroyed by a huge wave.

The Universal Declaration of Human Rights (1948) is a **United Nations** (UN) document. It lists the rights and freedoms of all the world's people.

The UN logo is recognized throughout the world as a symbol of peace and human rights.

Peace Corps' volunteers offer all types of aid, such as these medical supplies for people on the Yasawa Islands in Fiji.

diverse
different and varied

universal
affecting all people in the world

United Nations
an organization that promotes peace, security, and cooperation between countries

Peace Corps

In 1960, Senator John F. Kennedy asked students at the University of Michigan to think about serving their country in times of peace. He challenged them to volunteer overseas to help people in poorer countries. The following year Kennedy, as U.S. president, set up the Peace Corps (above, right).

The Peace Corps' goal is to promote world friendship and understanding. Peace Corps' volunteers range from college students to retired people. They work on many different projects. More than 190,000 Americans have served in 74 countries around the world since the program began.

Values to Live By

Imagine living in a community where people did not respect each other or would not tolerate different points of view. It would not be a very happy place to live. Civic values, such as respect and fairness, are important qualities for people to have in a democracy. These values help create a sense of what it means to be American.

Citizens who are loyal to the democratic principles and values of the United States are called patriotic. It is easy for citizens to say they are patriotic. They also need to show this through their actions. The democracy of the United States will be in safe hands if citizens can work together with their communities for the benefit of all.

Civic Value Checklist

✔ Do you respect people in positions of authority (for example, your parents and police officers)? [Respect]

✔ Do you treat everyone as equals? [Equality]

✔ Do you help out other members of your community? [Common Good]

✔ Do you accept differences in language, dress, food, race, and religion? [Diversity]

✔ Do you allow others to follow their beliefs? [Tolerance]

All new citizens of the United States say a special oath. They promise to support and defend the Constitution and the laws of the nation.

CASE STUDY

Agreeing to Disagree

The individual rights and freedoms that U.S. citizens enjoy come with responsibilities. People are free to express their opinions. However, it's important for them to also think about how their words might affect other people.

Citizens are also free to come together to protest about an issue. They have a duty to do this in a way that respects others' rights. People in a democracy often have different views about how things should be done. Our nation is designed to allow for these differences. Meanwhile, the shared duties and values of citizens help hold the diverse country together.

Responsibilities

Democratic principles and values help shape what it means to be an American citizen. Democracy: Responsibilities looks at some of the ways people can meet their democratic duties and make a positive difference in the world at the same time.

1. Voting is one way people can get involved in the political process. Using Democracy: Responsibilities as a reference, list three other ways.

2. Who was César Chávez? What did he do to make a difference in other people's lives?

3. Volunteers make an amazing contribution to the United States and to world society. Consider an issue in your community that you feel strongly about. It might be an environmental issue or a social issue (for example, pollution or poverty).
   - In what ways could you help to raise awareness about this issue in your community?
   - Describe a time when someone volunteered to help you or your family— or when you volunteered to help others.